Francis Frith's
AROUND BAKEWELL

PHOTOGRAPHIC MEMORIES

Francis Frith's
AROUND BAKEWELL

◆

Dennis Needham

FRITH
BOOK Co

First published in the United Kingdom in 2000 by
Frith Book Company Ltd

British Library Cataloguing in Publication Data

Around Bakewell
Dennis Needham
ISBN 1-85937-113-2

Frith Book Company Ltd
Frith's Barn, Teffont,
Salisbury, Wiltshire SP3 5QP
Tel: +44 (0) 1722 716 376
Email: www.frithbook.co.uk or info@frithbook.co.uk

Printed and bound in Great Britain

CONTENTS

FRANCIS FRITH: *Victorian Pioneer*

FRANCIS FRITH, Victorian founder of the world-famous photographic archive, was a complex and multitudinous man. A devout Quaker and a highly successful Victorian businessman, he was both philosophic by nature and pioneering in outlook.

By 1855 Francis Frith had already established a wholesale grocery business in Liverpool, and sold it for the astonishing sum of £200,000, which is the equivalent today of over £15,000,000. Now a multi-millionaire, he was able to indulge his passion for travel. As a child he had pored over travel books written by early explorers, and his fancy and imagination had been stirred by family holidays to the sublime mountain regions of Wales and Scotland. 'What a land of spirit-stirring and enriching scenes and places!' he had written. He was to return to these scenes of grandeur in later years to 'recapture the thousands of vivid and tender memories', but with a different purpose. Now in his thirties, and captivated by the new science of photography, Frith set out on a series of pioneering journeys to the Nile regions that occupied him from 1856 until 1860.

INTRIGUE AND ADVENTURE

He took with him on his travels a specially-designed wicker carriage that acted as both dark-room and sleeping chamber. These far-flung journeys were packed with intrigue and adventure. In his life story, written when he was sixty-three, Frith tells of being held captive by bandits, and of fighting 'an awful midnight battle to the very point of surrender with a deadly pack of hungry, wild dogs'. Sporting flowing Arab costume, Frith arrived at Akaba by camel seventy years before Lawrence, where he encountered 'desert princes and rival sheikhs, blazing with jewel-hilted swords'.

During these extraordinary adventures he was assiduously exploring the desert regions bordering the Nile and patiently recording the antiquities and peoples with his camera. He was the first photographer to venture beyond the sixth cataract. Africa was still the mysterious 'Dark Continent', and Stanley and Livingstone's historic meeting was a decade into the future. The conditions for picture taking confound belief. He laboured for hours in his wicker dark-room in the sweltering heat of the desert, while the volatile chemicals fizzed dangerously in their trays. Often he was forced to work in remote tombs and caves where conditions were cooler. Back in London he exhibited his photographs and was 'rapturously cheered' by members of the Royal Society. His reputation as a photographer was made overnight. An eminent modern historian has likened their impact on the population of the time to that on our own generation of the first photographs taken on the surface of the moon.

VENTURE OF A LIFE-TIME

Characteristically, Frith quickly spotted the opportunity to create a new business as a specialist publisher of photographs. He lived in an era of immense and sometimes violent change. For the poor in the early part of Victoria's reign work was a drudge and the hours long, and people had precious little free time to enjoy themselves.

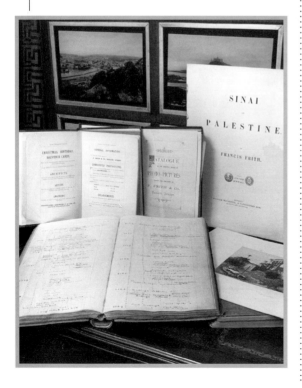

Most had no transport other than a cart or gig at their disposal, and had not travelled far beyond the boundaries of their own town or village. However, by the 1870s, the railways had threaded their way across the country, and Bank Holidays and half-day Saturdays had been made obligatory by Act of Parliament. All of a sudden the ordinary working man and his family were able to enjoy days out and see a little more of the world.

With characteristic business acumen, Francis Frith foresaw that these new tourists would enjoy having souvenirs to commemorate their days out. In 1860 he married Mary Ann Rosling and set out with the intention of photographing every city, town and village in Britain. For the next thirty years he travelled the country by train and by pony and trap, producing fine photographs of seaside resorts and beauty spots that were keenly bought by millions of Victorians. These prints were painstakingly pasted into family albums and pored over during the dark nights of winter, rekindling precious memories of summer excursions.

THE RISE OF FRITH & CO

Frith's studio was soon supplying retail shops all over the country. To meet the demand he gathered about him a small team of photographers, and published the work of independent artist-photographers of the calibre of Roger Fenton and Francis Bedford. In order to gain some understanding of the scale of Frith's business one only has to look at the catalogue issued by Frith & Co in 1886: it runs to some 670

pages, listing not only many thousands of views of the British Isles but also many photographs of most European countries, and China, Japan, the USA and Canada – note the sample page shown above from the hand-written *Frith & Co* ledgers detailing pictures taken. By 1890 Frith had created the greatest specialist photographic publishing company in the world, with over 2,000 outlets – more than the combined number that Boots and WH Smith have today! The picture on the right shows the *Frith & Co* display board at Ingleton in the Yorkshire Dales. Beautifully constructed with mahogany frame and gilt inserts, it could display up to a dozen local scenes.

POSTCARD BONANZA

◆

The ever-popular holiday postcard we know today took many years to develop. In 1870 the Post Office issued the first plain cards, with a pre-printed stamp on one face. In 1894 they allowed other publishers' cards to be sent through the mail with an attached adhesive halfpenny stamp. Demand grew rapidly, and in 1895 a new size of postcard was permitted called the

court card, but there was little room for illustration. In 1899, a year after Frith's death, a new card measuring 5.5 x 3.5 inches became the standard format, but it was not until 1902 that the divided back came into being, with address and message on one face and a full-size illustration on the other. *Frith & Co* were in the vanguard of postcard development, and Frith's sons Eustace and Cyril continued their father's monumental task, expanding the number of views offered to the public and recording more and more places in Britain, as the coasts and countryside were opened up to mass travel.

Francis Frith died in 1898 at his villa in Cannes, his great project still growing. The archive he created continued in business for another seventy years. By 1970 it contained over a third of a million pictures of 7,000 cities, towns and villages. The massive photographic record Frith has left to us stands as a living monument to a special and very remarkable man.

Frith's Archive: *A Unique Legacy*

FRANCIS FRITH'S legacy to us today is of immense significance and value, for the magnificent archive of evocative photographs he created provides a unique record of change in 7,000 cities, towns and villages throughout Britain over a century and more. Frith and his fellow studio photographers revisited locations many times down the years to update their views, compiling for us an enthralling and colourful pageant of British life and character.

We tend to think of Frith's sepia views of Britain as nostalgic, for most of us use them to conjure up memories of places in our own lives with which we have family associations. It often makes us forget that to Francis Frith they were records of daily life as it was actually being lived in the cities, towns and villages of his day. The Victorian age was one of great and often bewildering change for ordinary people, and though the pictures evoke an impression of slower times, life was as busy and hectic as it is today.

We are fortunate that Frith was a photographer of the people, dedicated to recording the minutiae of everyday life. For it is this sheer wealth of visual data, the painstaking chronicle of changes in dress, transport, street layouts, buildings, housing, engineering and landscape that captivates us so much today. His remarkable images offer us a powerful link with the past and with the lives of our ancestors.

TODAY'S TECHNOLOGY

Computers have now made it possible for Frith's many thousands of images to be accessed almost instantly. In the Frith archive today, each photograph is carefully 'digitised' then stored on a CD Rom. Frith archivists can locate a single photograph amongst thousands within seconds. Views can be catalogued and sorted under a variety of categories of place and content to the immediate benefit of researchers. Inexpensive reference prints can be created for them at the touch of a mouse button, and a wide range of books and other printed materials assembled and published for a wider, more general readership - in the next twelve months over a hundred Frith local history titles will be published! The

See Frith at www. frithbook.co.uk

10

day-to-day workings of the archive are very different from how they were in Francis Frith's time: imagine the herculean task of sorting through eleven tons of glass negatives as Frith had to do to locate a particular sequence of pictures! Yet the archive still prides itself on maintaining the same high standards of excellence laid down by Francis Frith, including the painstaking cataloguing and indexing of every view.

It is curious to reflect on how the internet now allows researchers in America and elsewhere greater instant access to the archive than Frith himself ever enjoyed. Many thousands of individual views can be called up on screen within seconds on one of the Frith internet sites, enabling people living continents away to revisit the streets of their ancestral home town, or view places in Britain where they have enjoyed holidays. Many overseas researchers welcome the chance to view special theme selections, such as transport, sports, costume and ancient monuments.

We are certain that Francis Frith would have heartily approved of these modern developments, for he himself was always working at the very limits of Victorian photographic technology.

THE VALUE OF THE ARCHIVE TODAY

Because of the benefits brought by the computer, Frith's images are increasingly studied by social historians, by researchers into genealogy and ancestory, by architects, town planners, and by teachers and schoolchildren involved in local history projects. In addition, the archive offers every one of

us a unique opportunity to examine the places where we and our families have lived and worked down the years. Immensely successful in Frith's own era, the archive is now, a century and more on, entering a new phase of popularity.

THE PAST IN TUNE WITH THE FUTURE

Historians consider the Francis Frith Collection to be of prime national importance. It is the only archive of its kind remaining in private ownership and has been valued at a million pounds. However, this figure is now rapidly increasing as digital technology enables more and more people around the world to enjoy its benefits.

Francis Frith's archive is now housed in an historic timber barn in the beautiful village of Teffont in Wiltshire. Its founder would not recognize the archive office as it is today. In place of the many thousands of dusty boxes containing glass plate negatives and an all-pervading odour of photographic chemicals, there are now ranks of computer screens. He would be amazed to watch his images travelling round the world at unimaginable speeds through network and internet lines.

The archive's future is both bright and exciting. Francis Frith, with his unshakeable belief in making photographs available to the greatest number of people, would undoubtedly approve of what is being done today with his lifetime's work. His photographs, depicting our shared past, are now bringing pleasure and enlightenment to millions around the world a century and more after his death.

BAKEWELL – *An Introduction*

THE TOWN OF Bakewell likes to be known as 'the capital of the Peak District'. Attractively located in the valley of the river Wye, it is surrounded by limestone: it is hard to believe that this area was once a tropical sea. Fossils prove that this region was part of a great ocean, and that these limestone deposits were made during the carboniferous period, some 286 million years ago.

There is some evidence that the Romans founded Bakewell. From then on, there are scant signs on the ground of any real civilisation developing during the Dark Ages. However, in 920AD the town seems to have been the location of a grand gathering. It was here that Edward the Elder, son of Alfred the Great, held a council: a host of warring factions were invited, including Scots, Northumbrians, Danes and Norsemen.

It was at this gathering that we first see the emergence of England as an entity rather than as a conglomeration of squabbling tribes. Edward was proclaimed 'Father and Lord' of the Anglo-Saxon lands, and was within an ace of being the first true King of England. The Danes at York and factions in Cumbria and Northumberland still resisted

the call for unification. Bakewell's place in the history books was assured. By the time Edward's son Athelstan took the throne in 924AD, England was already starting to get common laws, a coinage and the beginning of a civil service.

For this relatively accurate information we have to thank the Anglo-Saxon Chronicle, which was first compiled during the reign of Alfred and was maintained (with some gaps) for the next two hundred years. This has been a priceless record of that period in history immediately before the Normans arrived. Athelstan granted Bakewell's first charter in 926AD. Other charters were granted to nearby villages at Hope and Ashford-in-the-Water. This would seem to indicate a rather wealthy area in these pre-Norman times. 150 years later, when Domesday was compiled, lead mining was mentioned, a fact that probably accounts for the wealth. In the Domesday Book the town was referred to as Badequella, and it was also noted that a lead smelting site was located there.

During the reign of Henry III, in 1254, the market in Bakewell was formalised when a grant of a weekly market and a fifteen-day fair was made. The market as we know it today started in 1330. A cattle market has also been held here, and continues to this day. It was the cause of some controversy in the late 1990s when a £12m development took place, providing a modern agricultural centre, community facilities, a supermarket and homes for local people. Somewhat modernistic in design, it certainly clashes with what was there before. But it can be argued that the town was starting to stagnate; in time, this development will probably come to be accepted. Perhaps the most obvious clash is the new bridge spanning the river a few yards below the old stone one. This is a classic contrast of architectural styles: an elegant stone bridge versus a metal single span - the sort of thing the army might throw across a gap during tank manoeuvres.

One delightful feature of Bakewell, and a thoroughly historic one at that, is the annual ceremony of well dressing. This takes place towards the end of June each year; although the tradition was only revived here in 1971, wells were dressed in Bakewell back in the 17th century. The origin of this peculiarly Derbyshire custom is a mystery - although there are many theories. Well dressing was probably a pagan form of thanksgiving for a water supply. Before we all had piped water to our homes, the only place to set up a settlement is where there was water. If this dried up, life became untenable; therefore, giving thanks seemed a sensible thing to do. Today, five wells are dressed. The decorations are made by creating a large framework of wood into which clay is worked. Flowers, petals - in fact anything natural - is then used to create a picture. They are taken to the site and blessed by a local preacher.

Bakewell's original flirtation with well dressing was to publicise the efforts to create a spa in the town. Bakewell has a spring which feeds water into the Bath House at a constant 59 degrees Fahrenheit in both summer and winter. This Bath House was built by the Duke of Rutland in 1697: the idea was to compete with Buxton, but it was never really a success.

But if Bakewell is known for nothing else,

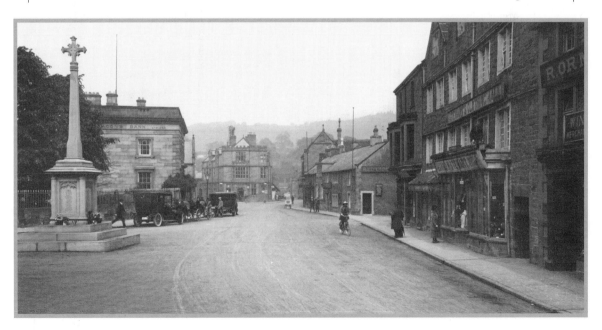

its fame is for ever assured by a small item of pastry: the Bakewell Tart. In fact, this nomenclature is incorrect. The item concerned is a Bakewell Pudding, and was actually created by mistake. It was at the Rutland Arms Hotel in the 1850s that the mistress of the hotel, Mrs Greaves, gave instructions to her cook to prepare a pudding. But instead of stirring an egg

'Pride and Prejudice', which was published in 1813. It is suggested that the town of Lambton in the novel is actually Bakewell.

Today, Bakewell is a thriving market town and location of the head offices of the Peak District National Park. This was the very first national park established under The National Parks and Access to the Countryside Act of

mix into the pastry, lining a bowl with the mixture and filling it with jam, our hapless lady lined the bowl with pastry, put in the jam and then added the egg mix on top. Despite the error, the resultant product turned out very nicely, and the recipe was preserved. Subsequently, it became quite popular, especially when a shop was opened in The Square in 1859, selling puddings made to the original recipe. Try this delicacy when you visit: it is still on sale.

The Rutland Arms is also noted as the place where Jane Austen stayed when she visited the town in 1811. Whilst here, it is believed that she was at work on her novel

1949. The Park itself came into being in 1951. This was as a result of a report by John Dower, a rambler and national park enthusiast. He was asked to provide a report on how this idea - already in use in other countries - could be adapted for use in England. There are 542 square miles in the Park, some forty miles from north to south and twenty miles across at its broadest.

The biggest event of the year in Bakewell is the Show. This takes place in August, and is a hugely popular event. If you are not planning to attend when it is on, avoid the town: the traffic is horrendous. There really is only one way to see Bakewell properly: on foot.

The endless small alleys and the steep hills with old houses and venerable buildings are fascinating. The tourist office is in Bridge Street, housed in the Old Market Hall, one of the many fascinating old buildings you will encounter. There, amongst a mass of varied information, you can collect the Town Trail and Map. This gives you a comprehensive plan of the town with many of the older places listed. In addition, there is a detailed description of a short walk around the town. This is about a mile in length, and the leaflet advises you to allow an hour. But if you have even the slightest interest in your surroundings, the walk can take double that. You will stop in one place to examine a particular building, and in another as you recognise one of the pictures in this book, and everywhere to admire the views. After all, Bakewell is not a place to rush around. Treat it as a vintage claret to savour and to enjoy at leisure, not as a Beaujolais Nouveau to be consumed quickly before moving to the next course.

In addition to the Trail, there are seemingly an infinite number of alternative places to wander, to discover and to explore. Try walking south along the river bank towards the Rutland Recreation Ground. Just below the main bridge there are always a flock of gregarious ducks demanding to be fed. But after admiring the gorgeous colours of the mallard, look at some of the other types. Several rarer ducks are often in residence, appreciating the chance of an easy meal rather than having to forage for food. Then check beneath the surface. Inured to constant disturbance in the water, huge trout swim languidly below the ducks' feet, also feeding on the crumbs that sink before a beak can get to them. These fish have also grown fat on the generosity of Bakewell residents and visitors.

But it is the essentially unchanging nature of Bakewell that gives it much of its appeal. It is most interesting to discover the locations that our cameramen have used over the century since their first visit to Bakewell. With just a little care, it is possible to find exactly where they stood. Then, study the photograph and see how much - or, more often, how little - has changed during the intervening years. It is a fascinating exercise, guaranteed to absorb everyone.

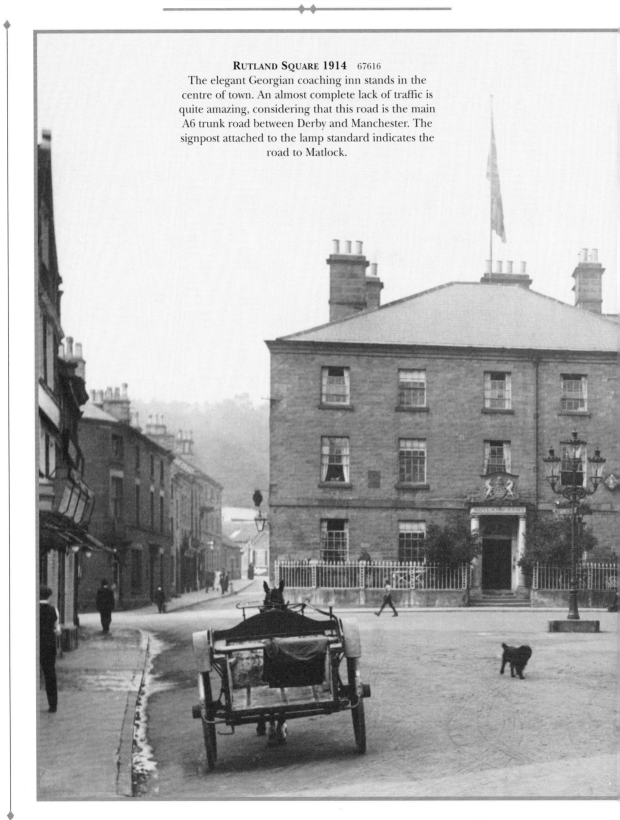

RUTLAND SQUARE 1914 67616
The elegant Georgian coaching inn stands in the centre of town. An almost complete lack of traffic is quite amazing, considering that this road is the main A6 trunk road between Derby and Manchester. The signpost attached to the lamp standard indicates the road to Matlock.

THE RUTLAND HOTEL 1923 73887
Nine years after photograph No 67616, many changes are clear to see. Motor vehicles are now in evidence, and the War Memorial has been built; it was erected to honour Bakewell's dead in the 1914-1918 war.

THE SQUARE c1955 B6003
Over thirty years later, horse traffic has disappeared, as have the ornamental iron railings to the right. They were almost certainly taken for scrap to help the war effort fifteen years earlier. Now, the War Memorial has got a proper traffic island around it.

THE SQUARE c1955 B6023
The trained climber on the hotel wall, only partly grown in the previous view, has now developed along the front wall. Bakewell Show is still held each August, a major event in the town.

THE RUTLAND ARMS HOTEL c1955 B6086
Taken later in the year, the Rutland Arms shows off its floral decorations. It was opened in 1804, and Jane Austen stayed here in 1811 whilst writing the early chapters of 'Pride and Prejudice'. Note that the traffic island has been further developed with 'Keep Left' signs added.

RUTLAND SQUARE 1923 73889
The view looks along Bridge Street towards the river.
The Original Bakewell Pudding Shop is located
further along on the right hand side. Stewarts
Clothing Hall is the major building on the right. Cars
and a horse-drawn vehicle are parked on the left in an
area that is now a bus stop.

THE SQUARE c1955 B6011

The War Memorial has been landscaped and protected from traffic, but the 'Keep Left' bollards are a few months away from installation. Beyond the parked car to the right is the tourist office and market place. Monday is Market Day in Bakewell. On the right, Burgons was a pre-supermarket groceries and provisions supplier. Butter was cut from a huge slab, sugar was weighed into stiff blue bags and biscuits also came loose - weighed out from large square tins.

THE SQUARE c1955 B6045

This view was taken from the Rutland Arms Hotel. Hulley's, a local coach firm, have one of their vehicles parked on the bus stand. Their stage carriage service reached - and still does - some of the more remote villages in the area. The bank is now operated by The Royal Bank of Scotland. On the right, the Red Lion proudly displays its AA and RAC accreditation.

RUTLAND SQUARE c1955 B6054

The Red Lion can now be seen to sell Tennant's Ales. Originally based in Sheffield, they were taken over by Whitbread's and the site is now closed. The unusual truck is built to carry lime, extensively quarried in this area. Note the appearance of an early form of television aerial on the chimney to the right.

BRIDGE STREET c1955 B6009
This view looks towards the town. Whilst still recognisable today, there have been many changes: volumes of extra traffic and street lights are just a couple. The lonely car on the left carries local registration marks, -RA being allocated to Derbyshire County Council.

THE GARDENS c1955 B6105
These gardens were laid out in 1814; to this day they are a small haven of peace away from the bustle of this busy market town.

BATH GARDENS c1955 B6083
Here we see these delightful gardens from a different angle. There is a small Garden of Remembrance here, together with one of the town's wells. The Bath House is behind, with its chalybeate spring producing water at a constant temperature.

GENERAL VIEW c1955 B6050
An overview of the town. The bosky slopes of the Wye valley are particularly clear in this view.

GENERAL VIEW c1955 B6049
Here we see another view of the Wye valley. Again, trees and attractive small fields give a vivid impression of the glorious nature of the Derbyshire Peak District.

THE RECREATION GROUND c1955 B6047
The Recreation Ground is located to the south of the town, close to the river Wye. The slopes of the valley create a wonderful feeling of space.

THE RECREATION GROUND c1955 B6026
With rose beds, trees and the river Wye on its boundary, it is small wonder that this is such a popular place. Today, the seats are even more popular than they were nearly half a century ago.

DAGNALL CLOSE GARDENS c1955
This is a more modern part of town, off the A6 to the south. The stone-faced houses are well in keeping with the rest of Bakewell. The road on the top of the hill - indicated by the houses - leads to the delightfully named Conksbury Bridge in gorgeous Lathkill Dale.

ST ANSELMS SCHOOL c1955
This school, on Stanedge Road, still exists today. The only real change has been the construction of the headmaster's house to the right hand side of this view.

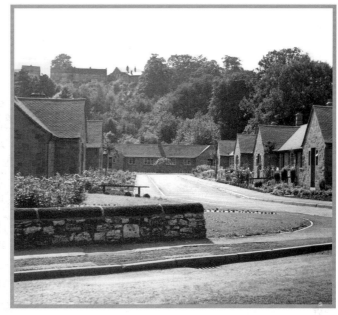

DAGNALL CLOSE GARDENS c1955 B6040

ST ANSELMS SCHOOL c1955 B6021

OLD COTTAGES 1914 67617
This row of delightful cottages is on South Church
Street, the hill out of town. The gas street light on the
left is now replaced by an electric one. The church is
almost completely concealed behind the trees.

SOUTH CHURCH STREET c1955 B6008

This view is taken from an almost identical view point as photograph No 67617, 41 years later. The lack of change from the previous shot is quite remarkable, considering there have been two world wars and a social revolution between.

HOLME HALL 1923 73895

Close to the banks of the Wye above the town, Holme Hall was built in the 17th century as a private residence, a function it performs to this day. A clear view of the elegant architecture can be obtained from the narrow lane to the front , roughly where the photographer stood.

HOLME HALL 1923
Here we see another view of this superb building, this time showing a more expansive view of the gardens and tennis court.

◆

THE MEMORIAL HOSPITAL 1923
Built as a memorial to the casualties in World War 1, this building on Butts Road has been added to quite extensively. Today, instead of being a hospital, it is now known as Bakewell Cottage Nursing Home.

HOLME HALL 1923 73894

THE MEMORIAL HOSPITAL 1923 73893

BRIDGE HOUSE 1923 73892

Alongside the river, close to the bridge, this building has now lost its croquet lawns. Once part of the council offices, today it houses Paxtons Restaurant downstairs and a bed and breakfast above. The gardens are open at all times and can be accessed from the riverside walk

FROM CASTLE HILL 1914 67613A

From the height of Castle Hill, close to the old railway line on the east side of the valley, Bakewell looks exactly what it is: a pretty and compact market town. The Wye is in the foreground of this photograph.

THE CHURCH FROM THE SOUTH WEST 1890 24627
The complex shape of the beautiful church of All Saints is shown to full effect in this view. The octagonal tower
was built in 1841 to replace the original 14th-century spire.

THE CHURCH, CHOIR EAST 1890 24629
This view of the interior clearly shows the quality of the misericords on the choir stalls to both left and right. Beautiful carving is a feature of this church. To the left of the altar, the tablet displays the Lords Prayer, and the Ten Commandments are to the right.

THE CHURCH, DOROTHY VERNON'S TOMB 1890 24630
Dorothy Vernon lived at Haddon Hall during the 16th century and eloped with John Manners, son of the Earl of Rutland. Being the last in line, she inherited the Hall, which then became part of the Rutland estate when the Manners family was ennobled.

THE CHURCH, THE VERNON CHAPEL 1890 24632
The Vernons acquired Haddon Hall in around 1170 and, along with the dukes of Devonshire, were one of the principal families hereabouts.

VIEW FROM YELD ROAD 1894 34252
From high up on Yeld Road, the parish church makes
an interesting study. Compare this view with the next
two, taken in later years, and note the changes -
or lack of them.

GENERAL VIEW 1923 73886

30 years after photograph No 34252, little has altered apart from the growth of trees. However, the cottage nearest the camera has had some of its foliage removed.

GENERAL VIEW c1955 B6020

Again, there has been little change from the previous photograph. It is quite remarkable how over 60 years can pass with so little alteration to the topography. Again, the nearest house is conspicuous. The remaining bushes have gone, and the walls have acquired a nice bright coat of paint.

THE CHURCH c1955 B6082

THE CHURCH c1955 B6082
This view of the church is taken from South Church Street, probably within the garden of what is now the house Braeside.

◆

THE CHURCH 1923 73903
Our final view of this delightful building was also taken from South Church Street, this time from a little lower down at its junction with Church Hill, the lane to the left. Note that both road and footpath surfaces leave much to be desired.

THE CHURCH 1923 73903

THE BRIDGE 1894 34254

The ancient - and only - river crossing for vehicles in Bakewell is illustrated here. The five-arched bridge dates from the 13th century, although it has been widened and improved down the years.

THE BRIDGE 1923 73884

Inevitably, there has been no change in the actual bridge, but the reeded margins closest to the camera have all been cleared away. The elegant cutwaters speak volumes for the bridge-builders' art.

THE BRIDGE c1955

Another bridge view, this time taken from the west bank, nearest Bakewell. Towards the far bank, the river is full of mallards, all demanding a sandwich with menaces. It is the same today, except that there are even more mallards, together with Canada geese and tufted ducks.

THE BRIDGE AND THE RIVER c1955

Here, the excellent footpath on the west bank can be seen. The path extends south right to the recreation park, and to the north, by crossing the bridge to the right hand bank, into the area known as Scot's Garden at the foot of Castle Hill.

THE BRIDGE c1955 B6104

THE BRIDGE AND THE RIVER c1955 B6024

THE RIVER c1955 B6093

This view shows the river to the south of Bakewell, around the Granby Court area. The recreation ground is in the distance. Note that even then a board prohibiting cycling was prominent.

DOROTHY VERNON'S BRIDGE, HADDON HALL c1955 B6033

South of Bakewell, the river runs through elegant parkland that forms the grounds of Haddon Hall. In this view, the lush nature of this wonderful valley is clearly illustrated.

DOROTHY VERNON'S BRIDGE c1955
This photograph focuses on the actual bridge, a pretty little footbridge a few yards south of the main bridge from the A6 trunk road into Haddon Hall. Dorothy Vernon's tomb can be seen in the church.

◆

THE OLD PACKHORSE BRIDGE c1955
North of Bakewell, an ancient packhorse bridge crosses the water. For centuries, lines of horses would lumber over this bridge weighed down with freight. Often, lead would be the main load. Before the advent of proper roads and even railways, these animals were the main means of transport; the well-worn tracks they navigated still exist today, although ramblers are the main users now.

DOROTHY VERNON'S BRIDGE c1955 B6035

THE OLD PACKHORSE BRIDGE c1955 B6039

THE PACKHORSE BRIDGE OVER THE RIVER WYE c1955 B6059
This view looks across the water meadows towards Bakewell. The worn stone bears mute testimony to the clop, clop of a million horses' hooves over the years.

THE OLD PACKHORSE BRIDGE 1923 73896
Here we see the Packhorse Bridge from downstream, with a clear indication of the speed of the water hereabouts.

VIEW FROM HOLME BRIDGE 1914 67620
This view looks upstream from the Packhorse Bridge. The view today, over 80 years on, is little changed, except that the wall to the right has largely disappeared.

VIEW FROM THE BRIDGE 1923 73898
A beautifully tranquil scene as the river Wye eases its way through Bakewell. The photographer took up his position on the 13th-century road bridge and pointed his camera south towards Haddon Hall. The path to the right is already surfaced: it was clearly well used in those days, as it is today. The gate into Bridge House gardens can be seen on the right.

THE RIVER WYE 1923 73899
Looking towards Bakewell bridge, the camera captures
some quite magical reflections. The wooded area in
the centre is a small island created as the river picks its
way through the town.

THE RIVER WYE C1955 B6005
The trees and vegetation on the far bank make this an archetypal English setting. This view is taken to the south of the bridge in Bakewell.

THE RIVER WYE AND THE BRIDGE 1955 B6004
The triangular cutwaters were shaped thus so that at road level they created a refuge in which people could stand as horses crossed the bridge. Today, they are a pleasant place to stand and take in the view without obstructing other pedestrians.

VIEW ON THE WYE 1914 67622
The river has several delightful waterfalls and weirs along its course. Some are quite tiny, while this example is one of the more spectacular ones.

RIVERSIDE WALK AND RIVER WYE c1955 B6027
A final view down the Wye, taken from the ancient Bakewell Bridge. The island we saw earlier is now plain to see on the left.

CHATSWORTH HOUSE c1885 18642
This is one of the great stately homes of England.
Owned by the Duke of Devonshire, it is built on a
grand scale. The bridge in the foreground is the main
entrance to the house; the water is the Derwent, en
route to its confluence with the Wye south of Rowsley.

CHATSWORTH HOUSE c1955 B6121

This view was taken 70 years after photograph No 18642, and apart from the statuary missing from the bridge buttresses, the scene is timeless. By the time this photograph was taken, the cost of running these great houses was such that they had to be opened to visitors. Chatsworth House dates from 1687,

EDENSOR, THE VILLAGE c1960 E130006

This place is an anachronism. For years, it used to be within sight of Chatsworth House, until the 6th Duke decided it spoilt his view. Thus, it was demolished and rebuilt here, one mile away, in 1839. The church is by Sir Gilbert Scott (1867) and the whole village is entered through a gate.

ROWSLEY, THE PEACOCK INN 1886 18617
The unsurfaced, muddy and rutted road here is now the A6 London to Scotland trunk route. Fashions have altered more than somewhat, and the outer wall of The Peacock looks much the worse for wear. The Midland Railway station was located to the right of this picture.

ROWSLEY, THE BRIDGE AND PEACOCK INN 1904 5216
This is yet another of the fascinatingly beautiful bridges that span the river Wye. A few yards below this bridge, the river empties into the Derwent en route to the Trent, the Humber, and eventually the North Sea.

HADDON HALL c1955 B6037

A distant view taken from the west, with the A6 trunk road in the foreground. This picture gives a wonderful impression of the beautiful location of this venerable building, home of the Duke of Rutland. Haddon Hall is popular with film-makers, having featured in Franco Zeffirelli's 'Jane Eyre' and the ITV series 'Moll Flanders'.

HADDON HALL c1955 B6036

This view shows the fortified appearance of the west front. When the Hall was built, King John refused permission to create a crenellated battlement, which would have made it militarily defensible. The Vernons added the battlements much later, when houses such as this did not need to be defended. To the right is the tower of the chapel. Inside, every period of Haddon's long history is represented.

HADDON HALL c1955
This is the Lower Courtyard. The uneven steps and stone flags have been worn by the feet of centuries. You can reach most of the buildings that make up Haddon Hall from here.

◆

HADDON HALL c1955
This view shows the main entrance. The North-West Tower is some 50ft high, and was built by Sir George Vernon around 1530. He was the last Vernon, for he had no male heir when he died in 1567. Haddon Hall passed to the Manners - later Rutland - family via his daughter Dorothy.

HADDON HALL c1955 B6030

HADDON HALL c1955 B6029

HADDON HALL, THE GARDENS c1955 B6031
The gardens of Haddon Hall are simply a delight, falling in a series of terraces from the house down to the river. They were originally designed in the early 17th century, but the actual plantings have changed somewhat.

MONSAL DALE c1955 M221012
Upper Monsal Dale is seen here from the Monsal Head Hotel. In breathtaking splendour, the river picks its way through the valley. The old railway line is visible in the distance.

MONSAL DALE, THE VIADUCT FROM MONSAL HEAD HOTEL c1955 M221013
A tiny locomotive heads over Monsal Viaduct towards Bakewell - probably heading for the engine shed at Rowsley. This was the Midland Railway main line from London St Pancras to Manchester Central. When it was opened, the company advertised this area as 'Little Switzerland'. The line closed north of Matlock and south of Chinley in 1968. Central station is now Manchester's G-Mex Centre.

MONSAL DALE c1955 M221015

Another nostalgic picture of steam in the Peak District. It has gone now: but for how long? A private steam company has already opened six miles of track north of Matlock, and intend one day to get right through to Buxton. With views like this at every turn, it will be incredibly popular. The viaduct, built in 1863, is a Listed Structure.

MONSAL HEAD VALLEY FROM THE HOTEL c1955 B6014

This more expansive view of the valley conveys a feeling of peace and beauty. This could be shattered by the passage of trains: the cutting started on the extreme left, running alongside and above the river.

MONSAL DALE c1955 M221066

This picture gives another impression of the wonderful feeling of space engendered by the Peak District. There was once a railway station to serve this little community, although most of the trade was visitors arriving - the actual tickets sold were few in number.

MONSAL DALE, MONSAL HEAD HOTEL c1955 M221016
The Monsal Head Hotel is a landmark around these parts. After the railway closed, the National Park bought the track bed in 1980 and created the eight-mile-long Monsal Trail. The railway enters a tunnel immediately after crossing the viaduct, and this is not open. Walkers are then routed past the hotel.

MONSAL DALE, MONSAL HEAD HOTEL c1955 M221018
The Monsal Head Hotel is a popular stop with walkers and motorists out to enjoy the sheer delight of this area. Like the Red Lion in Bakewell, this was also a Tennant's tied pub.

BUXTON ROAD 1923 73901
Running north from Bakewell, this is the main A6 and a dramatic drive. Following the Wye valley for several miles, it then climbs steeply towards Taddington before plunging dramatically downhill to rejoin the river again. The road has not been improved very much today.

LATHKILL DALE 1914
Of all the varied attractions of the Peak District, this one is up towards the top of the list. It was designated a National Nature Reserve in 1972, and is home to a wonderfully diverse collection of flora and fauna. Ash, wych elm and beech trees line the valley to augment this glorious spot.

LATHKILL DALE 1914
Limestone rocks are a major part of Lathkill Dale. Fortunately, it is possible to appreciate all of this river on its near five-mile journey from Lathkill Head Cave until it empties into the river Bradford at Alport: a footpath follows the whole course of the dale, making a simply wonderful exploration.

LATHKILL DALE 1914 67625

LATHKILL DALE 1914 67623

OVER HADDON, LATHKILL DALE c1960 O77001
Another aspect of the delightful river Lathkill. A short way downstream from this vantage point, the photographer would have crossed Conksbury Bridge, a suitable sturdy name to match the timeless charm of this scene.

MONYASH, THE CHURCH c1955 M222021
This tiny village of only a few hundred souls comes to life over the Spring Bank Holiday when, since 1974, the village has dressed its Newton Well.

EYAM, THE VILLAGE 1896 37812
Here we see the main street, with a group of villagers watching the photographer in action. Their clothing is typical of the era. A sign attached to the gable of the left hand building offers 'Good Stabling'.

EYAM, PLAGUE COTTAGES 1910 69211
Pronounces Eem, this is 'the plague village'. In the middle ages, bubonic plague was discovered in the village. Under the leadership of their vicar William Mompesson, the villagers isolated themselves, thus containing the spread of this killer disease which was responsible for the death of over a third of Europe's population at that time. Over 80% of the villagers perished, including Mompesson's wife. Note the children at play: all wearing hats.

STONEY MIDDLETON, THE CHURCH c1955 S452025
Completely overlooked by the towering limestone cliffs of Middleton Dale, the village church of Stoney Middleton is one of the few completely octagonal churches in England.

TWO DALES, RED HOUSE c1955 T206014
This small settlement to the south of Bakewell lies between Halldale and Darley Dale and, architecturally at least, has little to commend it. But this evocative picture of a Morris Minor saloon and a Triumph TR sports car in day-to-day use - rather than museum pieces - will stir many a memory.

ASHFORD IN THE WATER, THE DAY'S WORK DONE c1955 A324001
A sight from a different era, now gone for ever. A farm horse is led to the river Wye in Ashford for light refreshment after a day's work in the fields.

ASHFORD IN THE WATER, OLD COTTAGES c1955 A324002
These old buildings give a typical view of the village as it was then - and as it is today. Indeed, little has changed, save the re-routing of the main road that ran through the centre.

ASHFORD IN THE WATER, TOP PUMP c1955 A324017
This is one of six locations in the village where well dressing is carried out. For those interested in this ancient art, the dates co-incide with those at Monyash, mentioned earlier.

CALVER, CLIFF COLLEGE c1950 C399130
Here we see the stern exterior of Cliff College, with that most archetypal English game of croquet being played on the lawns. Located on the main road between Calver and Baslow, the college was built a hundred years ago and still functions today.

CALVER, CLIFF COLLEGE c1950 C399010
This ivy-fronted view of Cliff College is an altogether softer image than the previous one. The college, owned by the Methodist church, is home to some 70 lay students who study evangelism. The courses last from one term to three years. Graduates from Cliff can be found all around the world.

CALVER, THE VILLAGE c1950 C399045
A much-changed scene greets today's visitor to this spot, although the essentials are still in place. The Eyre Arms pub is still a Mansfield tenancy, although the brewery has recently been taken over. The filling station still exists, and there is another one opposite. The road layout has been radically improved.

BASLOW, THE VILLAGE c1955 B484006
This charming village on the river Derwent is dominated by the grounds of Chatsworth House. This section of the area is the old village known as Nether End. Newer parts to the north - Over End and Bridge End - are not quite so attractive. The Standard (?) car is registered in nearby Sheffield

BASLOW, THATCH END c1955 B484020
Recently renewed, the thatch on this row of cottages is exquisitely neat and tidy. Thatch is not a common roofing material in these areas; stone or slate tiles are much more usual.

GREAT LONGSTONE 1919 69206
Sweeping views of the wilds of the Peak
District are encapsulated in this picture.
Note the dry stone wall in the foreground.
This is built without mortar: each stone is
carefully selected to bind with its neighbour
to create a stock-proof barrier.

Index

Frith Book Co Titles

Frith Book Company publish over a 100 new titles each year. For latest catalogue please contact Frith Book Co.

Barnstaple	1-85937-084-5	£12.99
Blackpool	1-85937-049-7	£12.99
Bognor Regis	1-85937-055-1	£12.99
Bristol	1-85937-050-0	£12.99
Cambridge	1-85937-092-6	£12.99
Cambridgeshire	1-85937-086-1	£14.99
Cheshire	1-85937-045-4	£14.99
Chester	1-85937-090-X	£12.99
Chesterfield	1-85937-071-3	£12.99
Chichester	1-85937-089-6	£12.99
Cornwall	1-85937-054-3	£14.99
Cotswolds	1-85937-099-3	£14.99

Northumberland & Tyne and Wear	1-85937-072-1	£14.99
North Yorkshire	1-85937-048-9	£14.99
Nottingham	1-85937-060-8	£12.99
Oxfordshire	1-85937-076-4	£14.99
Penzance	1-85937-069-1	£12.99
Reading	1-85937-087-X	£12.99
St Ives	1-85937-068-3	£12.99
Salisbury	1-85937-091-8	£12.99
Scarborough	1-85937-104-3	£12.99
Scottish Castles	1-85937-077-2	£14.99
Sevenoaks and Tonbridge	1-85937-057-8	£12.99
Sheffield and S Yorkshire	1-85937-070-5	£14.99
Shropshire	1-85937-083-7	£14.99
Southampton	1-85937-088-8	£12.99
Staffordshire	1-85937-047-0	£14.99
Stratford upon Avon	1-85937-098-5	£12.99
Suffolk	1-85937-074-8	£14.99
Surrey	1-85937-081-0	£14.99
Torbay	1-85937-063-2	£12.99
Wiltshire	1-85937-053-5	£14.99

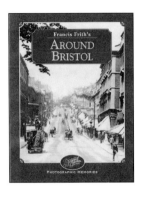

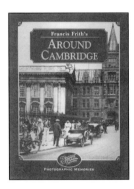

Derby	1-85937-046-2	£12.99
Devon	1-85937-052-7	£14.99
Dorset	1-85937-075-6	£14.99
Dorset Coast	1-85937-062-4	£14.99
Dublin	1-85937-058-6	£12.99
East Anglia	1-85937-059-4	£14.99
Eastbourne	1-85937-061-6	£12.99
English Castles	1-85937-078-0	£14.99
Essex	1-85937-082-9	£14.99
Falmouth	1-85937-066-7	£12.99
Hampshire	1-85937-064-0	£14.99
Hertfordshire	1-85937-079-9	£14.99
Isle of Man	1-85937-065-9	£14.99
Maidstone	1-85937-056-X	£12.99

British Life A Century Ago
246 x 189mm
144pp, hardback.
Black and white
Lavishly illustrated
with photos from the
turn of the century,
and with extensive
commentary. It offers
a unique insight into
the social history and
heritage of bygone
Britain.

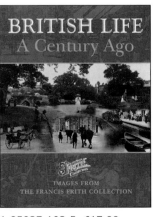

1-85937-103-5 £17.99

Available from your local bookshop or from the publisher

Frith Book Co Titles Available Soon

From 2000 we aim at publishing 100 new books each year. For latest catalogue please contact Frith Book Co

Bakewell	1-85937-1132	£12.99	Feb
Bath	1-85937-097-7	£12.99	Feb
Belfast	1-85937-094-2	£12.99	Feb
Bournemouth	1-85937-067-5	£12.99	Feb
Essex	1-85937-082-9	£14.99	Feb
Greater Manchester	1-85937-108-6	£14.99	Feb
Guildford	1-85937-115-9	£12.99	Feb
Harrogate	1-85937-112-4	£12.99	Feb
Hertfordshire	1-85937-079-9	£14.99	Feb
Isle of Wight	1-85937-114-0	£14.99	Feb
Lincoln	1-85937-111-6	£12.99	Feb
Margate/Ramsgate	1-85937-116-7	£12.99	Feb
Newark	1-85937-105-1	£12.99	Feb
Oxford	1-85937-096-9	£12.99	Feb
Oxfordshire	1-85937-076-4	£14.99	Feb
Shrewsbury	1-85937-110-8	£12.99	Feb
South Devon Coast	1-85937-107-8	£14.99	Feb
Southport	1-85937-106-x	£12.99	Feb
West Midlands	1-85937-109-4	£14.99	Feb
Around Leicester	1-85937-073-x	£12.99	Mar
Cambridgeshire	1-85937-086-1	£14.99	Mar
County Durham	1-85937-123-x	£14.99	Mar
Cumbria	1-85937-101-9	£14.99	Mar
Down the Severn	1-85937-118-3	£14.99	Mar
Down the Thames	1-85937-121-3	£14.99	Mar
Exeter	1-85937-126-4	£12.99	Mar
Folkestone	1-85937-124-8	£12.99	Mar
Gloustershire	1-85937-102-7	£14.99	Mar
Great Yarmouth	1-85937-085-3	£12.99	Mar
Kent Living Memories	1-85937-125-6	£14.99	Mar
Liverpool	1-85937-051-9	£12.99	Mar
Northumberland	1-85937-072-1	£14.99	Mar
Plymouth	1-85937-119-1	£12.99	Mar
Portsmouth	1-85937-122-1	£12.99	Mar
Southampton	1-85937-088-8	£12.99	Mar
Stratford upon Avon	1-85937-098-5	£12.99	Mar
Welsh Castles	1-85937-120-5	£14.99	Mar
Stone Circles & Ancient Monuments			
	1-85937-143-4	£17.99	Apr

Canals and Waterways	1-85937-129-9	£17.99	Apr
East Sussex	1-85937-130-2	£14.99	Apr
Exmoor	1-85937-132-9	£14.99	Apr
Farms and Farming	1-85937-134-5	£17.99	Apr
Horsham	1-85937-127-2	£12.99	Apr
Ipswich	1-85937-133-7	£12.99	Apr
Ireland	1-85937-181-7	£9.99	Apr
London	1-85937-183-3	£9.99	Apr
New Forest	1-85937-128-0	£14.99	Apr
Scotland	1-85937-182-5	£9.99	Apr
Sussex	1-85937-184-1	£9.99	Apr
Colchester	1-85937-188-4	£8.99	May
County Maps of Britain	1-85937-156-6	£19.99	May
Harrow	1-85937-141-8	£12.99	May
Leicestershire	1-85937-185-x	£9.99	May
Lincolnshire	1-85937-135-3	£14.99	May
Newquay	1-85937-140-x	£12.99	May
Nottinghamshire	1-85937-187-6	£9.99	May
Redhill to Reigate	1-85937-137-x	£12.99	May
Scilly Isles	1-85937-136-1	£14.99	May
Victorian & Edwardian Yorkshire			
	1-85937-154-x	£14.99	May
Winchester	1-85937-139-6	£12.99	May
Yorkshire	1-85937-186-8	£9.99	May
Berkshire	1-85937-191-4	£9.99	Jun
Brighton	1-85937-192-2	£8.99	Jun
Dartmoor	1-85937-145-0	£14.99	Jun
East London	1-85937-180-2	£14.99	Jun
Glasgow	1-85937-190-6	£8.99	Jun
Kent	1-85937-189-2	£9.99	Jun
Victorian & Edwardian Kent			
	1-85937-149-3	£14.99	Jun
North Devon Coast	1-85937-146-9	£14.99	Jun
Peak District	1-85937-100-1	£14.99	Jun
Truro	1-85937-147-7	£12.99	Jun
Victorian & Edwardian Maritime Album			
	1-85937-144-2	£14.99	Jun
West Sussex	1-85937-148-5	£14.99	Jun

FRITH PRODUCTS & SERVICES

Francis Frith would doubtless be pleased to know that the pioneering publishing venture he started in 1860 still continues today. More than a hundred and thirty years later, The Francis Frith Collection continues in the same innovative tradition and is now one of the foremost publishers of vintage photographs in the world. Some of the current activities include:

Interior Decoration

Today Frith's photographs can be seen framed and as giant wall murals in thousands of pubs, restaurants, hotels, banks, retail stores and other public buildings throughout the country. In every case they enhance the unique local atmosphere of the places they depict and provide reminders of gentler days in an increasingly busy and frenetic world.

Product Promotions

Frith products have been used by many major companies to promote the sales of their own products or to reinforce their own history and heritage. Brands include Hovis bread, Courage beers, Scots Porage Oats, Colman's mustard, Cadbury's foods, Mellow Birds coffee, Dunhill pipe tobacco, Guinness, and Bulmer's Cider.

Genealogy and Family History

As the interest in family history and roots grows world-wide, more and more people are turning to Frith's photographs of Great Britain for images of the towns, villages and streets where their ancestors lived; and, of course, photographs of the churches and chapels where their ancestors were christened, married and buried are an essential part of every genealogy tree and family album.

A series of easy-to-use CD Roms is planned for publication, and an increasing number of Frith photographs will be able to be viewed on specialist genealogy sites. A growing range of Frith books will be available on CD.

The Internet

Already thousands of Frith photographs can be viewed and purchased on the internet. By the end of the year 2000 some 60,000 Frith photographs will be available on the internet. The number of sites is constantly expanding, each focussing on different products and services from the Collection.

Some of the sites are listed below.

www.townpages.co.uk
www.icollector.com
www.barclaysquare.co.uk
www.cornwall-online.co.uk

For background information on the Collection look at the three following sites:

www.francisfrith.com
www.francisfrith.co.uk
www.frithbook.co.uk

Frith Products

All Frith photographs are available Framed or just as Mounted Prints, and can be ordered from the address below. From time to time other products - Address Books, Calendars, Table Mats, Postcards etc - are available.

The Frith Collectors' Guild

In response to the many customers who enjoy collecting Frith photographs we have created the Frith Collectors' Guild. Members are entitled to a range of benefits, including a regular magazine, special discounts and special limited edition products.

For further information: if you would like further information on any of the above aspects of the Frith business please contact us at the address below:
The Francis Frith Collection, Frith's Barn, Teffont, Salisbury, Wiltshire England SP3 5QP.
Tel: +44 (0) 1722 716 376 Fax: +44 (0) 1722 716 881 Email: uksales@francisfrith.com

To receive your FREE Mounted Print

Cut out this Voucher and return it with your remittance for £1.50 to cover postage and handling. Choose any photograph included in this book. Your SEPIA print will be A4 in size, and mounted in a cream mount with burgundy rule lines, overall size 14 x 11 inches.

Order additional Mounted Prints at HALF PRICE (only £7.49 each*)

If there are further pictures you would like to order, possibly as gifts for friends and family, acquire them at half price (no additional postage and handling required).

Have your Mounted Prints framed*

For an additional £14.95 per print you can have your chosen Mounted Print framed in an elegant polished wood and gilt moulding, overall size 16 x 13 inches (no additional postage and handling required).

---

* IMPORTANT!

These special prices are only available if ordered using the original voucher on this page (no copies permitted) and at the same time as your free Mounted Print, for delivery to the same address

---

Voucher for FREE and Reduced Price Frith Prints

Picture no.	Page number	Qty	Mounted @ £7.49	Framed + £14.95	Total Cost
		1	**Free of charge***	£	£
			£	£	£
			£	£	£
			£	£	£
			£	£	£
			£	£	£
			* Post & handling		£1.50
Book Title			**Total Order Cost**		**£**

Please do not photocopy this voucher. Only the original is valid, so please cut it out and return it to us.

I enclose a cheque / postal order for £ . . . .
made payable to 'The Francis Frith Collection'
OR please debit my Mastercard / Visa / Switch / Amex card

Number . . . .

Expires . . . .   Signature . . . .

Name Mr/Mrs/Ms . . . .

Address . . . .

. . . .

. . . .

. . . . Postcode . . . .

Daytime Tel No . . . .   Valid to 31/12/01

Frith Collectors' Guild

From time to time we publish a magazine of news and stories about Frith photographs and further special offers of Frith products. If you would like 12 months FREE membership, please return this form.

Send completed forms to:
The Francis Frith Collection, Frith's Barn, Teffont, Salisbury, Wiltshire SP3 5QP

The Francis Frith Collectors' Guild

Please enrol me as a member for 12 months free of charge.

Name Mr/Mrs/Ms . . . .

Address . . . .

. . . .

. . . .

. . . . Postcode . . . .

Free Print - see overleaf